T0276621

No Signal No Noise

Also by

A   JAMALI   RAD

and published by Talonbooks

for love and autonomy

still

NO SIGNAL

NO NOISE

Part 1 of The Self-Inscribing Machine series

A JAMALI RAD

TALONBOOKS

© 2024 A Jamali Rad

All rights reserved. No part of this book may be reproduced, stored in a retrieval
system, or transmitted, in any form or by any means, including machine learning
and AI systems, without the prior written consent of the publisher or a licence
from Access Copyright (the Canadian Copyright Licensing Agency). For a
copyright licence, visit accesscopyright.ca or call toll-free 1-800-893-5777.

Talonbooks
9259 Shaughnessy Street, Vancouver, British Columbia, Canada V6P 6R4
talonbooks.com

Talonbooks is located on xʷməθkʷəy̓əm, Sḵwx̱wú7mesh, and səlilwətaɬ Lands.

First printing: 2024

Typeset in Aglet Mono and Marco
Printed and bound in Canada on 100% post-consumer recycled paper

Cover image by A Jamali Rad

Talonbooks acknowledges the financial support of the Canada Council for
the Arts, the Government of Canada through the Canada Book Fund, and the
Province of British Columbia through the British Columbia Arts Council and the
Book Publishing Tax Credit.

Library and Archives Canada Cataloguing in Publication

Title: No signal no noise / A Jamali Rad.
Names: Jamali Rad, A, author.
Identifiers: Canadiana 20240422546 | ISBN 9781772016307 (softcover)
Subjects: LCGFT: Literature.
Classification: LCC PS8619.A45 N6 2024 | DDC C813/.6—dc23

Zero is invincible.
After all, it is *nothing* to begin with.

—Conradaxx

on Genius.com about The Smashing
Pumpkins' "Zero"

CONTENTS

PROLOGUE

If it is true that the intolerant violence of filiation was formerly buried in the sacred mystery of the root, and that entering into the opacity of this mystery was tragically granted, and if this opacity therefore both signified the mystery and simultaneously masked its violence – this always took place in function of a final underlying transparency in the tragic struggle.

—Édouard Glissant

Poetics of Relation
(translated by Betsy Wing)

Language is a system of sounds.

Language is a system of sounds that can be represented by a system of writing. A system of writing must have a purpose or some sort of meaning to it and have a set of symbols, which can be both written and read.

Language is a system of communication used by humans.

Language is a complex system of communication used by humans to convey thoughts, ideas, and emotions. It involves structured combinations of sounds, symbols, or gestures with shared meanings. It encompasses spoken and written forms, evolving through cultural and social interactions.

Language is a complex system, a formal representation of the world. It creates a logical structure for understanding one's surroundings.

Language is a systematic structure derived
from material forms of relation. Material
relations build forms upon forms of words,
symbols, and numbers that shape material
relations.

Language is a system of communication
formed by socioeconomic relations within a
given community.

Language is a social practice and is deeply
embedded in everyday activities and forms
of life.

Language exists only in relation.

Language exists only in relation and is a
product of historical material conditions,
emerging from the productive forces and
class struggles prevalent within a given
society. The ruling class, through their
control over the means of production,
shape language's form and content.
This linguistic hegemony obscures the
exploitation of the working class.

Language serves as a tool of ideological control, disguising the exploitative nature of the prevailing economic system. The ruling elite manipulates language, moulding it to propagate their values and norms.

Language is a construct of the ruling class. It is an instrument of ideological hegemony. It serves as a means of perpetuating the dominant ideas of the ruling elite, preserving existing power structures by asserting language as a static reflection of objective reality.

Language is imposed upon the proletariat by the bourgeoisie who, in controlling the means of linguistic production, shape consciousness and limit revolutionary potential.

Language, as controlled by the ruling class, disguises class conflicts and perpetuates false consciousness. The ruling class constantly alters language to meet their needs, while insisting on its fidelity to objective truth.

Language, as controlled and managed by the ruling class, is structured by writing.

Language is structured by writing, and writing provides a framework that can mimic, represent, reflect, or determine the ideological underpinnings for a given society.

Writing provides a structure, is a medium for propagating ideology.

Writing as a materialised form of structure serves as a means to represent, communicate, and manipulate numerical information.

The writing of numbers is essential for record keeping.

The writing of numbers, or mathematical notation, employs symbols and numerals to express abstract ideas, enabling the exploration of mathematical truths and the development of scientific theories.

The writing of numbers allows for a further abstraction in representing reality, an abstraction that does not rely on relational communication and can thus be used to supplement ideology as well as alter material reality.

The writing of numbers presumes a direct line to material reality, devoid of pesky relationality, and is thus used to ensure accuracy, traceability, and accountability.

The writing of numbers is used as a means to denote rationality, logos, or objective truth. However, numbers can only be understood with the help of language, that pesky relationality.

The writing of numbers, combined with ideologically bent language, allows the ruling class to shape understanding and guide future knowledge production. In this way, the ruling class skews the material world, furthering their ideology.

If language cannot be changed, neither can the conditions of the working class.

HOW TO DRAW A CIRCLE

Naming is a preparation for description.

—Ludwig Wittgenstein

Philosophical Investigations
(translated by G.E.M. Amscombe)

The following is an account of how it all started. Everything changed when I found the book.

It was a brisk morning, either late autumn or early spring, I can't remember. What I do remember is walking about through the uninhabited depths of narrow alleyways and on flat wastelands of crumbling sidewalks. A little disoriented or disengaged, I was still determining for what purpose I was out and about.

A day is like an unblooming flower upon which one may stumble, like, I assume, I did that day, upon a semi-ancient manuscript, a notebook of sorts, written by one who can only be called an obsessive, who, with little knowledge of mathematics, seems enthralled by the concept of Zero. I found myself immediately taken in by the mysteries of this number.

At first glance the text appeared to be some sort of linguistic exercise, wherein this semi-ancient (yet purely modern) monomaniac continuously pursues sources that they believe will lead them to the origin story of this admittedly complex entity.

I held the disordered pages of text between my hands, unable to know what to make of such a mess. Flipping through the pages, I landed on a random one and began to read.

Names for Zero

Śūnya (Sanskrit) is a word for void,
emptiness

Śūnyatā is a word for vacuity, nothingness

From Śūnya we go to Shifr, then Sefr, then
Cipher, then Zefirum, Psephos, Zeviro,
Zeuro, and finally Zero

I take my time as it comes and, as these things go, often forget to take note of my days. Suppose I purchased this crudely made book and took it home and, in this way, happened to awaken one morning with it having been placed upon my nightstand. Suppose I then pick up the book from its resting spot and begin to read the pages within, one page at a time, so as not to impress upon my mind too much of its strangely formed ideology too quickly. Suppose I do so and share that which I read with you, dear reader, so that you, too, may have access to these strange and muddled thoughts.

In a moment of history, a symbol appeared for Zero. It kept track of all the numbers, bushels of wheat, seeds, wool, of anything really. A symbol came and went, and came back again.

What happens when the body needs an absence to assert its own existence? What happens when Self is established in relation to an Other that is brought into being solely for the purpose of being in opposition?

A circle is drawn by a hand. One either exists inside or does not. But what happens if one does neither?

In my own way, I consider how I, too, can perhaps get a bit tangled in the thought of a singular subject. As the questions posed by the manuscript followed me through my day, I pondered the boundaries between Self and Other, being inside or outside of said boundary, and whether the possibility may exist to be at once both or neither inside and/nor outside.

I take a breath, slow and steady, filling in the crevices of my rib cage. I close my eyes and feel the emptiness opening inside my body, a felt lack.

There are times of which I have no memory, and there were times when I closed my eyes, then opened them only to find myself in completely unfamiliar surroundings.

I open my eyes now. Of course, from being just woken from slumber, my vision is still murky from being unused to being open as such. I look around to find the book on a table across the room. I immediately wrest myself out and reach out in a haste of anticipation to take hold of the book and flip through its pages.

The following is a list representing Zero
in accordance with Aristotle's *Categories*:

Zero has no substance

Zero has no body

Zero has no quality

Zero does not exist in time

Zero is not *in relation* to anything

Zero has no properties

Zero is not affected

Zero does not act as an agent of change

I am, at this realization, in astonishment of the stifling and limited philosophy, the abounding indignity of the exclusion of such a noble symbol.

I suppose it must have been a shock to a tame and stable system to introduce a symbol of such blatant contradiction. It contains within it at once nothing and everything; it is simultaneously infinitesimal and infinite, void and fullness, opacity and transparency. It is the knowable unknown.

I turn the page, look again at the loosely bound text.

Aristotle's system of logic is centred on the concept of identity:

A = A

From there, you move on to the Law of Noncontradiction, meaning two opposing states cannot be true at once:

not (A and not A)

Example: It is not true that it is both raining and not raining.

As stated in the *Prior Analytics*: "It is impossible that the same thing should be necessitated by the being and by the not-being of the same thing."

There is history on this ground, beneath the stifling weight of these wide glass windows and time-worn bricks. As regards the soothing storm booming in a near distance, my body, through the connection of my feet on the ground, settles onto the solidity of the hard floor as I close my eyes. Without a visual of the storm, I can only hear the raging tempest all around me: the slamming of the droplets from the sky, the bellowing wind travelling in a wave-like manner. I close my eyes as the thunderous vibrations pass through me.

Time passes as it always does, and upon opening my warmed and heavy eyelids, the storm seems to have now passed. I look out and across the window-covered walls as the wetted cement begins to dry out.

Kha is a word for place, used for the
position of a number, but also means
hollow, cave, cavern.

From kha we go to khak (dirt), to abq
(dust), to abacus (counting board), to
dhuli-karma (dust-work), and back to kha
(the hollow space left behind by the pebble
on a dust-covered counting board).

Feeling now a sort of curiosity about the materiality of the ground, with my calloused finger I trace the edges of pieces chipped away from the mortar. I trace the pockets of air speckled in the concrete wall that encases the space I now occupy.

And since, having fitted my flesh within these walls and at once managed to maintain a sort of tolerable body temperature, despite the lack of sunlight against my porous skin, as is often my inclination, I open upon a page of my book and, to my surprise, find a rather directly explicative statement following a rather untidy attempt at genealogy.

I suppose Nothing needs a chronicler, like anything else.

The concept of Zero, or the absence of
quantity, is fundamental to the history
of Zero, is inextricably linked to
the development of capitalist modes of
production, and the rise of the concept
of Zero has played a crucial role in
the development of numerical systems of
the historical context in which Zero
emerged and can be traced back to the
contradictions and tensions inherent in
a growing entanglement in the rise of
the binary system is closely tied to the
development of the kinds of technology
which enable more complex systems of
extraction of resources and labour.

Sometimes the obvious needs to be said:
the emergence of Zero reflects the material
conditions of the societies in which it
emerged.

It was, as I lay there in my place of residence, body limp like a seal splayed against a rock soaking up the rays of the sun, that I jostled myself out of my slumberous state and had the idea of moving out into the world. Perhaps it was the momentary slight change of light that offered an opening before the towering resurgence of perennial darkness. Perhaps it was the realization that I was not a seal and not soaking up warmth from a generous burning ball in the sky but sinking into a block of foam under layers of woollen textiles. Nevertheless, here I am now, book in hand, seated upon an austere wooden chair, awaiting wakefulness.

Being a thoughtful sort, I consider the ways in which I imagine these different stages of my being in and out of my body in various places, how my body expands and retracts through levels of relief.

Smudged and fogged, these windows as eyes for this narrow, long, and hollow room are no more ready for the day than my own, foggy and smudged and placed upon a similarly hollow head.

Before Zero was a number in Sanskrit,
there was the linguistic pause, elision,
an extension of a previous vowel, *avagraha*.

Exhausted with the world, I use the force of my body to wobble out of bed and turn on the light of a floor lamp in the corner of the room in which I sleep as the daylight is still too weak to make a difference. I blink my eyes a couple of times to adjust to their opening.

With a heavy head and heavy feet, I ask myself: What spaces occupy my sense of being in or out of place? What spaces hold presence and absence? What spaces are legible only through signs, measurements, grids? I look across the room at angles, the convergence of points, a perspectival marvel. All these spaces are in relation to my own form, a boundary in which I swell.

A sign is made legible in relation to
another sign, exists in relation to
nonexistence, is read only if it has
a form.

Any system of oppression begins with the
creation of boundaries. What is and what
isn't nestled within those prescribed walls
are then placed into discrete categories.

Placed within those walls is that which is
visible, knowable, describable by language,
can be bought and sold, is touchable.

Placed outside is that which is shrouded in
the darkness of the void and negation, is
unknowable and imperceptible.

Any system of negation begins with that
which is kept back in caged slit paper
thing after the records kept in the back
of time. A system is an apple. A system
is meaning cradled. A system is a body,
a prison-house for the soul, an enclosure.

I hold out my hand following the realization that the blood has at present raced away from my extremities. I begin a frail attempt to correct this, folding my fingers in and out to encourage movement by my lazy vessels.

Light bends its way through sheer curtains on the other side of the window. A wall is placed between my body and the light, with an opening, or doorway, through which I can see the shine of the hardwood floor reflecting the objects placed upon it: a bent metal bench, a bookcase, a planter with palms that sway against the shifts of air brought about by the open door.

My often-wavering attention moves around the room, landing here and there: a basket against the wall, a stool whose wiry legs resemble the outlined shape of a bell, an unused fan, a large metal tin used for the disposal of garbage, and eventually and inevitably back to the table in front of me, landing on the book I had recently placed there with my still-frosty fingers. Yes, the book with which I have been at present constantly preoccupied, this conceptually jumbled assortment of ideas about Zero. As is the case with my wavering attention, I realize now that I have yet to read it from the first page, so here I am, ready to begin.

Let us begin at the beginning.

Language arose out of the exchange of resources, and writing, out of accounting for those resources.

Before anything else was written, people had to account for goods received and given. The first systems of writing were used for counting and naming things. A hollow reed or wooden stylus was used to make impressions on the surface of moist clay tokens.

Beginning in the eighth millennium BCE, tokens with various shapes, with dots and sets of lines, both plain and complex, were used in the exchange of goods. Around 3,500 BCE, the clay tokens were perforated in order to be strung to a clay bulla, while others were kept in a sort of spherical envelope, which displayed on its surface (using those same dots and lines) what was contained within it, a sort of abstraction of abstraction. Writing was accounting, and accounting was a way of keeping track of how much of what came from whom and went where. Of what was there and no longer is, a record of what was and what is to come.

Writing was a promise.

The first systems of writing were a sort of money.

In this kind of system, there is only a representation of that which is, given or taken, positive or negative. In this system, there is no need for the number Zero.

As writing and record keeping evolved, the wedge shapes of cuneiform expanded into a complex system for words as well as numbers (written in positional notation). Still, there was no sign of Zero until, around five thousand years ago in Sumeria, someone came up with the idea of taking a couple of the wedge shapes and slanting them on a 45° angle, representing "nothing in this column."[1]

It is at this time that Nothing can begin its journey. As previously attested, once something is written, it comes into being.

---

[1]   Robert Kaplan, *The Nothing that Is: A Natural History of Zero* (Oxford: Oxford University Press, 1999), 12.

Thus begins our story, I thought to myself, readying my sapless mind for further study.

Zero first appeared in Sanskrit as a dot, or "bindu," which also means "globule" or "droplet."

This dot not only stood as a placeholder, or nothing, but also as the unknown or a variable. Both were viewed as an *unfilled container*.

In Hinduism, "void" or "nothingness" is never unqualified, but a receptivity. And "śūnya," meaning "nothing," comes from the root "svi," meaning "swelling"[2] or "swollen."[3]

2   Kaplan, 59.

3   *Wisdom Library*, "Shunyata, Śūnyatā: 19 definitions," accessed June 10, 2024, www.wisdomlib.org/definition/shunyata.

I stir up from my seat and head out into the shifting weather of the day: one moment a cold front, another, a warm sun-filled breeze. As I walk, I feel the sun blazing upon my flushed cheeks. At once this movement of my limbs must come to a halt, as the cold front, with its blazing winds and sudden downpour, has forced me to take cover. And so, book in hand, I head inside a little coffee shop to seek refuge and a warm beverage to comfort me.

As is often the case with such places, this particular establishment has been embellished with several quite random pieces of decor, as if a truck carrying goods to a flea market overturned and its wares somehow spilled indoors, and as one is wont to do resulting from such tragedies, the proprietors took it upon themselves to take in these orphaned pieces and thenceforth placed them ever so gently in various corners, on ledges, on stands, hanging them from the walls, and simply allowing them to sit about like patrons.

With my fullest effort, and despite my wavering relationality, I attempt to focus my attention on the book in my hand as the room, filled to the brim with trinkets, agitates my senses.

Plagued by negative definition, Zero is
defined by that which isn't, is non-being,
is unlife. It gives form to that which
does not exist. It names that which has no
name. It positions that which cannot have a
place.

Zero is absence, annihilation, the
privation of language, and the removal of
space and time.

Zero is lack embodied.

With my feet placed on the ground, I feel the force of gravity radiating up until it lands at the cuff of my ankles. Likewise, the hard seat of my chair presses against my body as I strain against my propensity to be a slinking mass spreading upon the manufactured form that means to hold my body in place.

I feel around with my body, keenly aware of the shapes that surround me. Parts of my body go in and out of awareness of their ability to process sensory information. Nevertheless, I am reminded of the multidimensionality of lived experience, my ability to be a multidimensional being interacting with multidimensional materiality.

I was comforting myself with the thought of the stability of my materiality when my attention opened upon the concept of Zero as a shape in space. I suppose that, like any other shape, Zero shifts and changes. Though these alterations are so slight, that one would never guess there were any changes made at all.

But immediately following these thoughts, I think to myself: what if the alterations weren't so slight, but done in such a way as to transform Zero's functional being altogether.

If you pinch the top of the Zero and twist it just a little, you get a sort of curved teardrop shape, reminiscent of a seed, a leaf, a feather, or a cypress tree.

Like pieces of a puzzle, two of these shapes can exist in a circle. A newly formed Zero containing two of its own altered forms.

The Aristotelian Law of Noncontradiction
states that a symbol cannot exist for
nothingness, as that would imply that
something would be equal to nothing,
in other words something = nothing.

As Zero is both *nothing* and a symbol,
therefore *something*, according to
Aristotle, it cannot exist.

It is true that I am absolutely enthralled by the generics of the concept of Zero, but what of its specific history? What of its origins in use? I frantically flip through the pages, hoping such an account can be found in this loosely assembled document, and land upon a page of delightful historicity.

In 1881 a farmer in the village of
Bakhshali in present-day Pakistan found an
ancient manuscript. When the text on the
bark was transcribed, it became clear that
it was a merchant text about mathematics.
This newly found text was found to be
littered with dots, dots that happen to be
the earliest form of Zero as known today,
a tiny circle on the number line.

Zero travelled from Babylon to India with
the Macedonian Alexander, and there it
intermingled with a pre-established concept
of the void, nothingness, śūnyata, and
the binary of creation and destruction as
personified in the god Shiva, who creates
the universe out of nothing from within an
infinite void.

On a shivering winter's night, as is perhaps often the case, in a language true of sounds, making use of its written form, I am of the mind to venture out, plunging into the night to feel the dampened air flail against the tightening of my skin, with my hands cold and retreating into the dark of my wetted sleeves. As I tease the written form, I know, book in hand, or rather, book bag, that I, too, should retreat into a warmed haven, where, upon entering the candlelit and secluded hall, I would open upon a page to read, again, to learn of Zero's history.

Beginning in the seventh century CE, the advance of Islam through Asia precipitated exchange with the Indian subcontinent, spreading Indian numerals and mathematics throughout the Muslim world. In the eighth century, the court of the second Abbasid Caliph Al-Manṣūr (754–775) received an embassy from Sindh, which included an astrologer who brought with him mathematical and astronomical texts, including those of Brahmagupta.

Brahmagupta's *Brāhmasphuṭasiddhānta* is probably the earliest known text to treat the concept of Zero as a number, rather than as simply a placeholder digit representing another number, as was done by the Babylonians, or as simply a symbol for lack of quantity, as was done by the Romans. As requested by Al-Manṣūr, Brahmagupta's work was translated into Arabic as *Zīj as-Sindhind*, by Al-Fazarī, Ibn Sa'd, and Al-Khwarazmi.

Born in the eighth century in Khwarazm, a
Central-Asian Iranic region, Al-Khwarazmi,
a polymath with an extensive body of work
in the fields of mathematics, astronomy,
and geography, lived in Baghdad, where he
learned from and expanded upon Greek and
Sanskrit texts on mathematics and geography
and Persian and Babylonian astronomy.

During the Crusades, despite the
destruction of libraries, among the
European soldiers' loot were many important
scientific manuscripts, which made their
way to Spain, and from there to the rest of
Europe.

Among them were manuscripts by
Al-Khwarazmi, whose treatise on solving
elementary equations (*Al-jabr wa'l
Muqabala*) was foundational for what came
to be known as algebra, and whose name,
latinized as "algoritmi," is the basis
for the term "algorithm." His book *Al-Jam'
wal-Tafriq bi hisal-al-Hind* (Addition
and Subtraction in Indian Arithmetic)
was translated into Latin, facilitating
Zero's introduction to Europe.

I drew a picture of nothing, now I can't seem to find it.

I place a
finger on
the page to
feel its
weight in
reverse
as if
gravity
could overcome
my

I place a
finger on the
page to feel the
outline pressure un-
pressed to feel
the fibres left
behind within the
valleys of
the terrain I
know as my
skin

I place a
finger on the
page to feel what
parts of me get
left behind
when I lift my
finger

I place a
finger on a
scale to read the
pressure of the
void our shadows touch
a wall fill
corners slip
into empty
space find
ways of
becoming
an undercurrent
absent emergence a
fleeting movement a
critical mass of
weightless
being if
all our shadows
could collide we
would take
over the

THINKING WITHOUT

KNOWING

One thinks that one is tracing the outline
of the thing's nature over and over again,
and one is merely tracing round the
frame through which we look at it.

—Ludwig Wittgenstein
Philosophical Investigations
(translated by G.E.M. Amscombe)

I must admit I went in search of something. At length I wandered streets, back alleys, looking inquisitively at piles of recycling, longingly into storefronts. I entered one such store at some point, with a heaviness in my heart, a sort of dread of future disappointment. I scanned shelves filled with books, new and old, piles of yet-to-be-organized books, carts filled with clearance books, and boxes of undesirable books being given away for free.

After all this, my unending wandering, it so happened that in such-and-such a box, with cardboard haggard and smelling of old pressed wood pulp, I found a small booklet filled with random scribbles, notes: a collection of short chunks of text. In front of my bewildered eyes was a text that seemed incomplete, thoughts that seemed to be left untied, a sort of assembly of fragmented ideas.

And yet it seemed to be exactly that for which I had been searching: an explanation. It seemed to me that the aim of this book was to provide a sort of description of the way things are and could be. So, as a way of getting where I want to go from the first kick, I start from the back of the book. A few pages in, I read:

The proto-Manichaean ancient religious concept of the duality of good and evil combined with the concept of Zero as a number makes way for the binary system of Zeros and Ones that creates the basis on which run supercomputers that manage and mediate all our interactions with ourselves and others.

After much prolonged sauntering, my legs stiffened in place, unable to move farther in their assumed voyage. Except, perhaps they would give way to entering a place of rest, with warm caffeinated beverages to invigorate my system for the remainder of the journey. I could not but overlook the warm fog of the interior as much opposed to the crispness of the air in which I was previously so braced. Perhaps the warmth of environs, if not the warmth of a beverage, will loosen the cramped muscles about my legs.

In such a place, I could have decided it to be indispensable to open upon a page of the book to which I have been so increasingly bound. Did I forget to mention that I took the book home from the shop? And that the more I read from it, the more engrossed I became with it? Well, that is what happened.

And so, here in this place, I prepare to settle in a cozy spot and once again engage in this text. I unbuckle the leather strap which had wrapped itself over and around the little book, holding the tattering pages in place, and I begin to gaze again upon a page.

Zero is disclosure
through the prism of ideology

and has nothing

to show for it

A historical context: today I awoke from a stupor that can only be described as interrupted. Perhaps sleep is a memory of prelife, the conditions of which follow you to your dream state, or lack thereof. I awoke to find trees toppled, objects strewn across streets, sidewalks, and backyards.

In this fragmented state of being in the world I am again pulled towards the Zero manuscript. As if the words of the text are in a way a reflection of the disarray in the material world of which I am a part, extended in time.

This is how the words are used.

Zero is both enclosure and disclosure.

Making nothing material, its form makes the
void manipulable.

Zero contains what was previously assumed
uncontainable.

Its coming to being makes everything
containable: land, bodies, behaviour,
desire, decisions, movements, time, memory,
absence, a forgotten lullaby, seven flights
of stairs and a broken elevator with
technicians on strike in the not-for-
profit senior housing, jaws hinging,
loading with spices and empty calories, a
sublime nothing, trembling yellowed leaves
in a swift breeze dropping, mulched, and
returned to earth.

Zero discloses through enclosing.

Following my deep contemplation and persistent, though often interrupted, study of the found book, I realize that Zero and One are not the architects of their roles, but that something else puts them in their places. This unseen force makes and erases boundaries, acts in the shadow, almost as if mechanically, without responsibility. Perhaps it was originated by some sort of ancient outsider that landed upon this hunk of rock, creating a set of rules, by order and ordering, a sort of categorization or classification of the inhabitants.

Systems of power define and bring into
light, create signs of that which they want
to make knowable and manipulable.

Systems of power create categories of Self
and Other, that which is outside of the
category of Self. One is designated as the
sign for Self, and Zero is made into the
sign for Other. In this very way, capturing
Zero, bringing it *into being*.

A category is a place no one ever mentions. Is also a thought, perhaps perhaps, perhaps so.

Like Zero, the Other changes over time, shifts like the movement of tectonic plates overtop the earth's mantle. But some old habits die hard, and as otherness in itself must be maintained, and, as the state of the world may be, this oppositional dance between Self and Other, who are forever returning to their primordial positions …

I drew a picture of nothing, and it looks like a hole.

emptiness
swells

and is
clothed in
form

I'm feeling
my way to
the pause
that closes
a thought

the
incandescent
darkness that

fills
emptied
fullness

Zero mocks
language builds
barriers around

nothing
makes
nothing

knowable taints
knowledge laughs at the
tools made for
enclosure adds

nothing
turns everything it
touches
into

NOTHING MAKES

There is no outside; outside you cannot breathe.

—Ludwig Wittgenstein

Philosophical Investigations
(translated by G.E.M. Amscombe)

I begin my days as I end them: in traces of shadows surrounding a vague memory of a shape. Sleep is a skill mastered only at death. In the time it takes to count time, I let myself fill space: on sidewalks, in bedrooms, in cafés, and in bookshops. I'm in a flea market, a gathering of forgotten wares: a chipped pot, a set of large spoons, a cedar chest filled with spools of scrap yarn, piles and piles of books upon piles of books.

A shape is a thing that is always present. It presumes presence. A shape makes anything real. Perhaps one can point to a thing and say, "This is a circle." Would that thing not be present to the viewer and would the utterance not make it legible to the interlocutor?

Someone points to a pile and says, "Look at that pile. Isn't it just this or that?"

A pile is a collection of shapes, all of which are present for the experiencer of such shapes and the collection of which they are a part.

Someone points to another pile. My eyes follow a gesture like a yellow jacket follows a sweet scent in the depths of summer. Upon landing on the collected shapes, my eyes trace the outline of each shape, to know its texture, its weight. But no, eyes cannot know those characteristics, only touch can interpret the fibres that contain a generalized shape. Only holding the object will transfer a feeling of weight.

In such-and-such a pile piled upon another, it would seem that I find a tattered perfect-bound assemblage of pages. I place the book in my hands and let it land, ragged and worn, on my skin. I trace its edges with my fingers, feeling its minuscule ridges. I breathe in the residue of its past travels. I breathe out the letters spelled out on the first page:

Z-E-R-O.

Naming is a memory for future utterance.

I hold the book and open it to a page towards the end, a little taken aback by the rather prescriptive nature of the words I read. Yet I find myself leaning into it, captivated by the thought experiment.

Picture yourself out in the world, a physical embodiment of absence.

Like any other day, I am out in the world. Within this sonic, visual, and textural environment, I think back to my previous reading of the book: the thought experiment.

As I walk around, I imagine my shape as absence made into matter, as if my body, as absence, has persisted in time. To think: what history unfolds in the ridges of my skin.

History, like anything, is written by someone.

Writing is the distinguishing factor
between history and prehistory. Word
for word, the writers of history, like
Narcissus, are enamoured by the reflection
of the Self, against the unwritten
unwritable Echo, the Other, the barbarian,
bound by mimesis, doomed to repeat only
what is reflected by the Self, and whose
body withers, leaving only the vocality of
the repetition.

I begin my days with declarative sentences, as the shufflings around of the day are unmuffled by my removal of wax earplugs and a cotton-lined band of cushioned cloth I wrap around my eyes, surrounded by layers of linen and wool coverings over my listless limbs, empty and yet heavy.

Perhaps this is why I am so enamoured by the found manuscript perhaps. A text devoid of itself, as if nothing needs to be said or written, but *is*, in a way, without saying or writing a thing.

Nemesis uses the tally sticks of moneylenders to keep the score, to balance the budget of fortune, of injustice and retribution, for deeds done and just deserts, to get to Zero.

Zero sometimes enters as a point between two sides. Not itself in opposition, but an equalizer, patiently and silently awaiting the score to be settled, to turn everything into nothing.

Zero is a destination.

Perhaps this body, my body, is more or less than just as much
as anything to be near asphalt darkened by rain, water pools.
Here, in this dampened air to be or sorted to be

constructive
constructed

\

In Maya culture, Zero is a simultaneity of the infinity expressed through the passage of time. Zero is the beginning and the end, the absence of quantity, and what holds the space between the past and the future.

In visual representation, Zero takes many shapes: at times a flower, a face, a closed fist, an eye, but most often a shape that some believe to resemble a seed or a shell, but is most likely a cacao bean or pod.

Zero: an absence of quantity, holds the space between one transformation to another. Zero, like money, holds no value.

Perhaps that is why the Maya chose to represent Zero with the image of what they used as currency: Cacao.

In the K'iche' Mayan language, "today" is expressed as "kamik," which literally translates as "death."

Zero, or "Nik," is the ending of one cycle and beginning of another.

The Maya view of time is cyclical, as seen in colloquial expressions: "Everything that has happened, will happen again" and "Every beginning will have an end, and every end will have a new beginning."[4]

Zero is not a destination, but a point of renewal.

4   J. Mucía Batz, "'Nik' – The Zero in Vigesimal Maya Mathematics," *Bulletin of the AAS* 53, no. 1 (January 2021), baas.aas.org/pub/2021n1i336p03.

My mind makes acute an awareness acutely aware of this
the similarities of my the text in the manuscript and my
own thoughts.

Could it be the words that have seeped deep into mine that
I no longer can distinguish?

To defeat an enemy, you must become like it.

Since finding the manuscript, Zero has taken over all my waking thoughts. I see Zero everywhere in all the things around, in the depths and surfaces of everything I ...

Being left completely to myself, I open upon a random page, again:

Zero began as an indexical
kept the other numbers in their place

Zero is the left-behind
the space of a removed pebble on a
counting board the

Zero is a

nothing happens

dirt

or sand

sad symbols for forgotten spots

empty like the

left behind

like the sort of thing you

can't remember the

Language made the symbols

To write, "

I am

ready

to be

counted"

Before there was writing, there were
imprints of hands on the interiors of
cave walls.

An originary

declaration of the Self

set forward

from despair with a

smattering of similitude in the

gathering storm

above, stars can see

everything

in the vacuum of

the space between One and

a distance as vast as a

seed planted and forgotten as a

charity auction as a

low-impact exercise routine as a

built barricade as a

literary archive as a

non-metaphorical speed bump as a

road blocked by rubble as a

pun not intended as a

compliant architecture as a

systematic or systemic

negation of the

can't feel a

can't stop a

body lost is a

body in

flux the material

cyclical nature of

time is

infinity in

being

nothing

Something felt more distant when it was right next to me.
Is this loneliness, an absent emptiness, a fullness removed?

A rock is still until it is moved, much like I am, perhaps, a
body in

space folded in upon until

I am.

I place my visual apparatus on the pressed pulp page, dried, ominous, and inked upon:

Have no despair, though you may be loath
to admit, Zero permeates your very being,
haunts your every step. It lurks in wait at
every corner of every decision and is at
once at the whim of chance, a disquietude,
which, as an ordinary contradiction, roars
over the calm waters of settlement.

My enemy's enemy is my enemy.

It is with a heavy heart that

I feel

falling

an empty my

a numbness perhaps

perhaps if I am without a body that enclosed perhaps without a body or piles of bodies once embodied vacuous now perhaps

perhaps there's something there perhaps there's nothing to it perhaps and perhaps shaking a tree for falling fruit or a body shaking is also a removal perhaps

perhaps a Zero amounts to nothing perhaps dead eyes dead vacant as the *s'got nothing up there* perhaps in a flash perhaps it was all for naught perhaps

Something appears to appear out of nowhere, where this and that are bound together in this forever othered of disparaging despair.

To forget is to remember negatively. I have hands and a head and they proceed in their own ways according to such and such a rule.

A history is unbound to its location when forgetting is prioritized over the material.

A tree is torn from the ground, paved over, and forgotten.

Something is set on fire.

Images are staged to distort reality.

People forget and are forgotten.

Moments proceed in their own way as they
always do. Channelling statistics is a
technology of populations in numbers.

Everything must be accounted for.
Everything must be bought and sold,
owned, or exchanged. Thus a feeling
is perhaps induced perhaps, a sort
of numerical sublime.

A moment arrives as any as a happy accident in which systems
create systems divide to divide to divide and

people create systems

It's just a happy accident that systems divide

that the systems created by

divide and

that the systems

create

people who divide

It's just a happy accident that I

create
created a happy that

nothing
is accidental

In my formation

a sort of

I twist to unfurl
and build the

assumption that
there are two
sides

upset with the
balance of relations
when people
read the
consequences of

when one encounter projects
onto another and a simple
pillage becomes
an ongoing present

and my skin, thinly
veiling an abject
vacuity spills
over into
every
aspect
of e
very
life

The cold has stiffened the ground outside as I articulate a
strategic or axiomatic multiplicity exists only because of me

My arms stretch out to retract

everything

I've come to know myself this way

now

in this cold air

in the absence of mountains and streams

in the absence of the dry desert air

when one encounter bleeds into the other

I exist there

on two land masses stretched over the ocean

I am the encounter that makes One definitive

my name is malleable

my name is shifting, unsaid or unknown

my name is

made up again and again

over and over

I articulate that which is

Because I am

, too

though nothing

with or without me

exists

In movement, is a vestige of

I am and *nothing* is

an absent *is* is

refuted recognition is

against memory is

a frame for otherness is

the outside within is

a transition between sense-image

and the "symbolic order of language"⁵ is

a place for the in-between is

a holder for the "not-" is

everything *other than* is

the systematically negated is

"this untamed nature"⁶ is

5   Christopher Bollas, introduction to *Freud and the Non-European*, by Edward
     Said (London: Verso, 2014),12.
6   Frantz Fanon, *The Wretched of the Earth*, trans. Richard Philcox (New York:
     Grove Press, 2004 [1963]), 182.

a landscape, a backdrop is

the *natural background to the human* is

the negation of *civilization*

seen through the scientific gaze is

far from an *inert thing* is

the potential of exponential is

a removal of the proverbial straw is

out of place is

dislodged or *exile* is

nothing in place of something is

something perhaps, could be is

the unity of *everything* and *nothing* is

in movement, the

enclosure of

negation that

permeates

is

I drew a picture of nothing, now it's over and done with.

SOURCES

Aristotle. *Prior Analytics*. Translated by A.J. Jenkinson. classics. mit.edu/Aristotle/prior.2.ii.html.

Batz, J. Mucía. "'Nik' – The Zero in Vigesimal Maya Mathematics." *Bulletin of the AAS* 53, no. 1 (January 2021). baas.aas.org/pub/2021n1i336p03.

Bollas, Christopher. Introduction to *Freud and the Non-European*, by Edward Said. London: Verso, 2014.Kaplan, Robert. *The Nothing That Is: A Natural History of Zero*. Oxford: Oxford University Press, 1999.

Fanon, Frantz. *The Wretched of the Earth*. Translated by Constance Farrington. New York: Grove Press, 1963.

Fanon, Frantz. *The Wretched of the Earth*. Translated by Richard Philcox. New York: Grove Press, 2004 [1963].

Kaplan, Robert. *The Nothing That Is: A Natural History of Zero*. Oxford: Oxford University Press, 1999.

Seife, Charles. *Zero: The Biography of a Dangerous Idea*. New York: Viking Penguin, 2000.

Wisdom Library. "Kha: 31 definitions." Accessed June 19, 2024. www.wisdomlib.org/definition/kha#sanskrit.

Wisdom Library. "Shunyata, Śūnyatā: 19 definitions." Accessed June 10, 2024. www.wisdomlib.org/definition/shunyata.

ACKNOWLEDGMENTS

This series began with research supported by the Conseil des arts et des lettres du Québec. This book was written with the support of the Canada Council for the Arts and the Ontario Arts Council. For their help with early conceptualizations of Zero, I would like to thank Rah Eleh, SF Ho, and Claire Lyke. And thanks to Ryan Fitzpatrick for his support and editing throughout the writing of this book and to Khashayar Mohammadi for their help with Latinization.

About The Self-Inscribing Machine Series

Beginning with the invention of Zero, The Self-Inscribing Machine is a speculative history of the binary and its prototypes. This series traces concepts of Self and Other as well as the mathematical, cultural, and philosophical foundations of the machines that drive the contradictions of capital.

A JAMALI RAD is a text-forward artist born in Iran and currently living on the Traditional Territories of the Attawandaron (Neutral), Anishnaabeg, the Haudenosaunee, and Lūnaapéewak Peoples. They have published two full-length books of poetry: *for love and autonomy* (Talonbooks, 2016) and *still* (Talonbooks, 2021). Their most recent work is the chapbook *WHAT I WANT* (Model Press, 2022). Jamali Rad also co-founded the journal *About a Bicycle* and the small poetry publisher House House Press.